Maria Dellos

Maria expressed a love for art as a child. In the 80's, she fell in love with the Southwest. Rubber stamping was new and exciting so like all stampaholics, Maria soon collected hundreds of stamps, ink pads and supplies.

Maria designed and taught for Ben Franklin Crafts in Tucson, Arizona, giving her the chance to share her talents. She is patient, detailed and teaches her secrets in classes and demos.

In 2001, Maria discovered gourds. For many years, gourd artists have used leather dyes as their coloring medium but the color fades. Maria discovered a Premium Ink Dye that does not fade and she fell in love with the quality, affordability and dynamic results.

Maria found that these ink dyes are rich in color, fade-proof, archivally safe and permanent on gourds. The result is ... superior process for cre ...

Maria brought the p ... Welburn Gourd Farm a ... launched a product line called GourdMaster Finishes. Maria is an artist for the farm, teaching and demonstrating.

Many thanks to my family and friends... Cheryl and Jann; Dan Weaver, owner of Ben Franklin Crafts in Tucson, Arizona; Andre Cox; Stewart Superior Inks; and Welburn Gourd Farm.

Maria presents live demonstrations on the internet at www.gourd.tv.

View more of her gourd art at www.mariasartcreations.com and at www.welburngourdfarm.com.

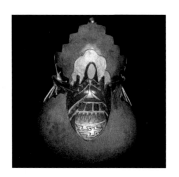

Maiden Gourd
page 7

Chief Gourd
page 9

Red Gourd Mask
page 19

Feather Medallion Gourd
page 22

Turquoise Necklace
page 23

Turtle Island
page 25

Gourd Urn
page 29

Stair-Step Gourd
page 34

Grecian Urn Gourd
page 43

Swirl Design
page 47

Lacework
page 49

Laced Gourd
page 50

Getting Started

Since there are many shapes and styles to choose from, consider a 5", 6" or 7" bottle gourd for your first one. Carefully examine the gourd for cracks and be sure it stands well balanced.

Notice the natural markings on the gourd caused by frost in the drying process; these markings add to the aesthetic beauty of your finished gourd.

You can buy gourds professionally cleaned or you can buy them "as is" and clean them yourself.

   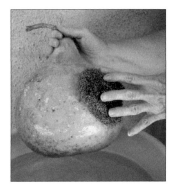

Basic Cleaning
for the Outside of a Natural Un-Cut Gourd

A professionally cleaned gourd is much easier to work with, but for those starting with a natural gourd, here are some cleaning suggestions:

• Fill a wash pan of water large enough to soak a gourd. Add 1 cap of bleach to 1 gallon of water.

• Soak gourd 10-15 minutes to soften the outside dirt and mold, rotating and immersing to wet the entire gourd.

• Use a copper pot scrubber to remove all the debris. Repeat soaking and scrubbing until it is clean.

• Let it dry before continuing or speed the process with a heat tool. Make sure it is completely dry.

• Some areas of the gourd may need sanding. Sand with a fine grit sanding block or sandpaper.

• After sanding, use a damp cloth to remove the dust. You are now ready for designing.

• Another cleaning method is to put your dirty gourds in a plastic trash bag and place it in the sun for several hours. The skin, dirt and mold will scrub off very easily. The sun will form condensation inside the bag, providing enough moisture to wet the gourd. This will not work in the colder climates, so you may want to follow the above soaking instructions.

 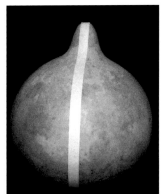  

Basic Marking
on Your Gourd with Masking Tape

Dark spots on the gourd surface are created by frost during the natural curing time. These spots add an interesting effect when adding color to your gourd.

Basic Taping

Divide the gourd in half with ½" masking tape, starting at the bottom center, bringing the tape to the top center.

Repeat the masking tape in the opposite direction, creating 4 equal areas of the gourd.

Cutting a Gourd Open

Many beautiful gourd designs are simply applied to the outside of an uncut gourd. You may want to create your designs on an uncut gourd and skip these steps altogether.

If you decide to cut your gourd, use a Heavy Duty Handle X-acto™ knife with the saw blade #227 to cut your gourd open, or use a small hand saw or a small power saw.

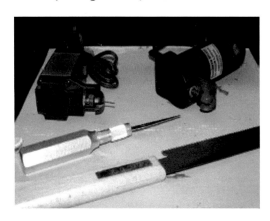

There are many tools available for cutting into your gourd, from hand tools to expensive power tools. I admit I own most of the fancy power tools, but I can never do without my Heavy Duty Handle *X-acto*™ knife with the saw blade #227.

Power tools are not always necessary to cut open your gourd but it does make it easier. The *X-acto*™' saw blade accomplishes the job quite nicely and eliminates the noise of a power tool.

The front hand saw is found at *Harbor Freight*. The Silver handle is a heavy duty hobby knife with a #227 saw blade. The power saw in the back left is from *www.micromark.com* and the power saw on the right is from *www. welburngourdfarm.com*.

TIP: Remember that saw blades and knife blades are sharp. Be careful when working with them, always direct the blade away from your body, and refer to any safety tips that come with the tools.

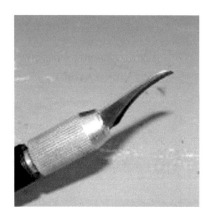

Another blade I use frequently is the #106 carving blade. These blades are very sharp so be careful. Always direct the blade away from your body.

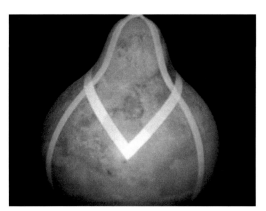

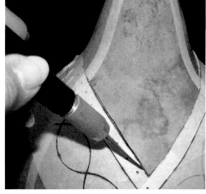

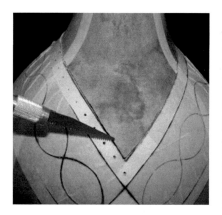

How to Cut a Gourd Open

Marking your gourd with a pencil line or with masking tape will make it easier to cut in the correct place. By using masking tape, you won't need to erase any lines, simply remove the tape.

Taping a "V" Line:

Create a "V" in the front of the gourd, rounding it to the back. This area can be cut out or left for further designing.

Instead of drawing pencil lines to design your gourd, use ½"- ¾" masking tape to map the area you are going to cut out.

This process works better and allows improved symmetry in the design. Even if you are doing freehand designing, taping helps in planning the design placement, especially if you are designing with geometrics.

TIP: Use a baby wipe instead of an eraser to remove pencil lines of your freehand design. You will not use an eraser again.

Cutting into a Gourd

Before you start sawing into your gourd, you need a sharp blade and a hobby knife.

Rock this blade into the area you wish to cut out. Rock it back and forth until you feel it has created a cut into the gourd.

Rock the blade out of the gourd and insert your saw blade.

Sawing into a Gourd

If you are using a power saw, carefully follow the instructions above before you begin sawing. Do the same when using a handsaw as this picture shows an x-acto saw blade #227.

You must rock the blade every time you change direction of the cutting.

TIP: Remember that saw blades and knife blades are sharp. Be careful when working with them, always direct the blade away from your body, and refer to any safety tips that come with the tools.

Cleaning the Inside of a Gourd

If you cut your gourd open, then you will want to clean the inside to remove seeds and make the surface smooth. Scraping debris from the inside of a cut gourd is a tedious but necessary job before you can continue to the next step.

TIP: Save the seeds to grow gourds next year. Plant them in full sun in early Spring, about March. (Your geographic climate may vary your planting season.)

Clean gourds outdoors. Empty the inside of the gourd frequently so you minimize the collection of debris flying up towards you.

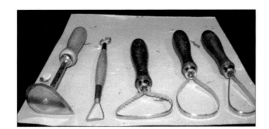

There are many scraping tools to choose from and usually you need more than one shape.

Each shape performs in a different way depending on the contour of the inside wall of your gourd.

Wear a dust mask to protect your lungs from the mold and dust spores inside of a gourd.

Ball Attachment

This scraping tool designed by the Welburn Gourd Farm is compatible with any power drill tool.

There are long and short shanks with course and fine grit ball tips. The ball tips are very strong and durable, capable of cleaning many gourds. Firmly grip your gourd securely in one arm, hold the power drill in the other. The drill will turn inside debris into dust in seconds.

If needed, finish cleaning with a manual scraping tool.

Scraping out the debris manually is time consuming. It can be hard on your hands and arms.

Although the cleaning ball attachment on the power drill is an amazing discovery, it does not replace the use of the manual scraping tools.

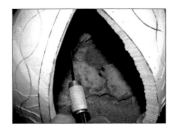
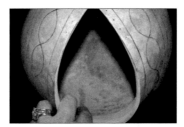

Clean the Opening

Use a carving blade #106 to carve the opening. Observe the left opening to see the difference. It is shaved and neater looking than the right side.

For a pleasing appearance, sand this area well after carving.

The inside and the opening edge have been cleaned.

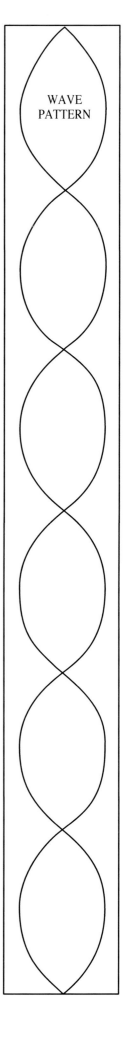

WAVE PATTERN

Transfer Patterns and Designs to Gourds

To begin, try a basic small gourd (or another design) to practice several techniques.
Stamp a design on your gourd or simply draw a design with a pencil.

Apply Design with a Rubber Stamp Design

Stamping directly on a gourd does not always work well, so I use the masking tape transfer process. I find that stamping on tape is the best way to get a complete stamped image.

Prepare Design - Using a roll of masking tape 2" or 3" wide, cover one side of an 8" x 11" or 5" x 7" acrylic/glass sheet, overlapping the tape at least ¼".

Ink the Stamp - Apply permanent ink or Permanent Black Ink Dye to a stamp.

Stamp an Image - Press the stamp evenly onto the tape and heat set until the ink is dry. This only takes seconds.

  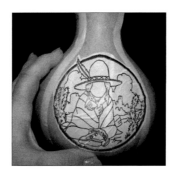 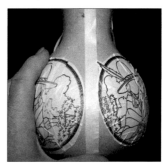

Apply Design to Gourd with Tape

Trim away excess tape, remove tape from the glass, then apply the pattern to the gourd.

Remove Tape with Design from the Glass

Carefully remove tape from the glass. Make sure you pull all the layers at the same time to prevent ripping. Cut around the image with an X-acto knife.

Trim Tape Around the Pattern

Apply directly to the gourd. You only need enough tape around your image to adhere it to the gourd.

Apply Tape to Gourd

Reposition the tape until you are satisfied, then press the tape in place and wood burn directly on the tape. This is a great technique I have shared with many people.

The tape technique is one of many useful ways to transfer and wood burn a design. It is very cost effective and convenient to use.

Another way to transfer a design is with Pyrography Paper. It is a transparent paper that is compatible with your home computer and printer. Print images from your computer; trim and tape in place on your gourd and wood burn directly on it.

TIP: Another item that works well with this technique is Press and Seal Wrap found in the grocery store. These techniques allow your hands free to wood burn your design and to see exactly where you are so there are no mistakes.

Add more Designs Around the Gourd

Center designs between tape so that designs go around the entire gourd. Add borders and decorative motifs between the designs and around the neck if desired.

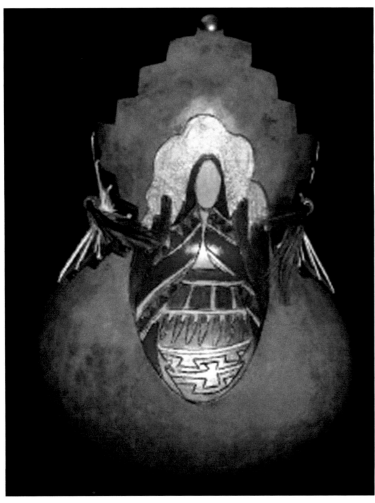

MAIDEN PATTERN - You may want to alter the stamp pattern slightly so it will work best on your gourd.

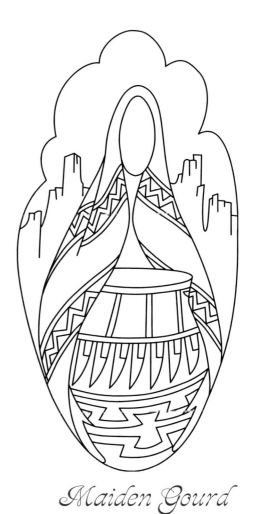

Maiden Gourd

Color this beautiful design, then add feathers and string to decorate the sides.

Indian Maiden stamp SS89 is from
IBrakeforStamps.com

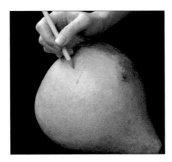
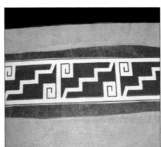

Optional Ways to Apply a Design

You can also draw directly on a gourd with a pencil, or transfer a design with Graphite paper, or a stencil.

Pencil

Use a 2B (soft) lead pencil to draw a design directly on a gourd. A Wet Wipe is perfect for removing pencil marks from the surface. TIP: A mechanical pencil will make consistently thin lines.

Graphite Paper

Place graphite paper on top of tape. Secure a paper design over the graphite with removable tape. Trace with a pencil. After tracing, hold the image in place and lift a corner carefully to check the transfer. When complete, remove the graphite paper. Cut off excess tape and carefully remove from glass, place on your gourd.

Stencil

Trace a stencil with a pencil directly onto the tape. Trim excess tape and place onto your gourd. Your craft stores have a variety of stencils to choose from and don't forget to check the sewing department for more geometric stencils.

CHIEF PATTERN
You may want to alter the stamp
pattern slightly so it
will work best on your gourd.

Chief stamp SS-82
is from *IBrakeforStamps.com*

Chief Gourd

*This is a great design to practice new techniques for designing
on gourds... cleaning, tracing, stamping, inking, finishing.*

Wood Burning

Incising with a hot tool works especially well on the soft woody surface of gourds, and creates a beautiful look.

Versa Tool by *Walnut Hollow* is a good beginner woodburning tool. It comes with several tips giving you flexibility in burning your design. Instructions with this tool give great ideas for the use of each tip. Practice on a piece of gourd to determine time and pressure needed to achieve an even design. Using too much pressure or holding the tip too long in one spot will burn too deep and could ruin your design.

The professional woodburning tool is the Detail Master Unit. It is one of the most popular woodburning units designed for gourd art. The pen tips are heavy duty and each has a unique purpose. Available at *www.welburngourdfarm.com*.

Sanding

Lightly sand the gourd surface with a fine grit sanding block or a Teflon pad to soften your burn lines.

Clean with a damp cloth and follow the coloring instructions.

If you want to carve or recess your design, then read the next step.

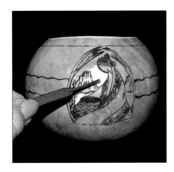

Chip Carving

Making a Recessed Design

When planning to wood carve, chip carve or recess a design, wood burn first and then carve or chip out the gourd.

This will prevent damaging the shell of the gourd and allows for smoother carving.

This step saves so much time and prevents the tools from slipping. Another reason for using this technique is to remove the area planned for in-laying embellishments such as stones, sand and beads.

A Dremel tool with sanding accessories will clean the carved area to a smooth finish and if you wish to use hand tools, a file and rasp are very effective. Practice on a piece of gourd first and then work on your art piece.

Once you have carved out the outer shell, you have exposed the raw porous gourd. Most people use acrylic paint to color this area but now you have another choice... GourdMaster Ink Dye mixed with GourdMaster Gourd Varnish. Mix about 1 tbsp. of gourd varnish with 10 drops of ink dye in a covered container. Use a paintbrush to apply this mixture onto the raw gourd area.

This mix air-dries quickly. It will dry in seconds with a heat tool. The mix can be stored covered for several weeks.

Remove Sticky Residue

Once your design is completely woodburned, remove all the tape. To remove any sticky residue, wipe clean with a cloth treated with an odorless paint thinner.

Lady stamp is from *IBrakeforStamps.com*

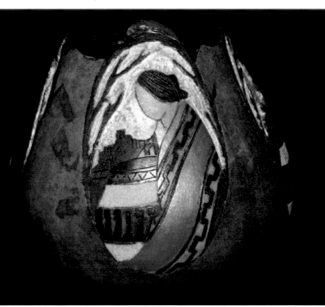

FLORAL DESIGN
You may want to alter the stamp pattern slightly
so it will work best on your gourd.

Stained Glass Floral Circle stamp is from *IBrakeforStamps.com*

Mix colors to create beautiful solid, metallic, mottled and natural finishes on this beautiful gourd.

Geometric Design on Gourd

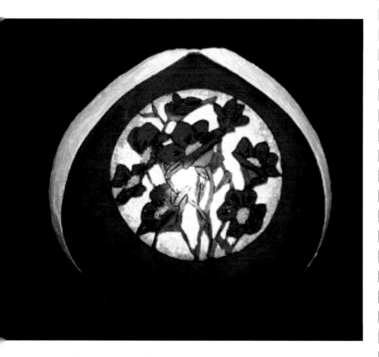

Floral Design on Gourd

Glowing ink colors highlight the beautiful floral design on this classic gourd.

This pattern is a rubber stamp. The gourd is wood-burned and the background is recessed.

Cherry Red Ink Dye and Old World White paint were used to color this gourd.

Finish the surface with *GourdMaster* Varnish to protect it.

GEOMETRIC stamp is from
IBrakeforStamps.com

Coloring with Inks

Permanent Ink Dyes are very concentrated... only a few drops will color a medium size gourd.

Permanent Ink Dyes from *GourdMaster* are alcohol free, fade resistant, acid free and archival safe, and very concentrated. Only a few drops will color a medium gourd.

If you use other permanent inks, be sure they are non-solvent inks. Ink dyes are not all permanent so choose carefully.

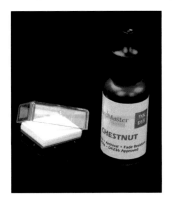  

This 1" cube applicator takes about 10 drops of ink when using it for the first time. As you use the ink, the color will weaken. When it does, add 2-3 drops of ink to replenish the pad.

For each color of ink, use an applicator specific for that color. With a Sharpie pen, write the color on the plastic lid and store upside down so the ink is at the top of the pad. When using the pad, rotate it so you use the ink on all sides.

If you are accustomed to working with leather dye, you will need to change your approach slightly for applying ink dye. Unlike leather dye, which dries very quickly (one of the reasons for the streaking problem), ink dye has a longer drying time. It is best to apply the ink in a circular motion, covering the area that is in front of you.

With a facial tissue, touch lightly to soften the ink and to blend, heat set with professional heat tool.

TIP: When you begin where you left off, make sure you have the same amount of ink in the pad so it will blend with the previous area. Use a tissue to blend. Heat set as you proceed from one area to the next. To minimize ink on clothing and hands, color in sections. You can always add another coat after drying the first application.

When wet, this ink can be cleaned up with water. When dry, ink remover is necessary. Alcohol does not work since there is no solvent in the ink.

Although ink dye is water based, its specific chemical make-up does not allow for dilution with water. Extender medium is compatible to mix with ink, slowing the drying time and giving the ink the ability to flow for decorative style painting.

Mix 1-2 drops of extender with 3 drops of ink. This mix is ideal for shading and dragging color. This ink will air dry, but speed drying with your heat tool for about 30 seconds sets the ink and allows you to continue without waiting.

For the larger areas of your gourd, use felt treated with a few drops of ink. Cut a piece of felt about 2" x 3" and fold it to slip into a clip. If you want to store this felt, leave felt on the clip, slip it into a baggie marked with the color name.

This keeps nicely. You will not get it on your hands because you will reach for the clip and not the felt.

Helpful Tools

A few helpful tools will make working with gourds easier.

These can often be found in your home, or you may want to purchase a few to make attention to details easier.

A microbrush is a great tool for very small intricate areas that other tools will not reach.

Use a pin drop of ink and touch the tip to a facial tissue to absorb the excess ink. Then color the intended area.

If you need to remove more ink or soften the color, use a clean microbrush to soften the area.

Wipe the tip of the brush with a baby wipe and these brushes will last a long time for repeated use.

Another useful tool for applying color is a cotton swab. They are inexpensive and apply ink very nicely, especially in curves and stems.

A dry swab will soften the ink just like using a tissue in larger areas.

Throw them out after use.

Recipes for Mixing Ink Dyes with Products

Mix colors and products to create and experiment with colors and finishes.

  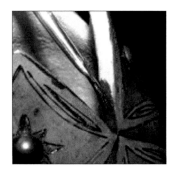 

Staining the Raw Surface of a Gourd

In a small mixing cup with a lid for storage, pour $^1/2$ oz. of varnish. Add ink dye 1 drop at a time until you get the desired depth of color. *GourdMaster* Varnish is a special varnish created for gourd art. This product is of the highest quality and does not yellow, crack or fade.

Mix well and with a paintbrush, paint the raw carved areas. This is great for adding color to a gourd where your products usually sink in and turn very dark. This mixture can be stored for weeks, covered; if it thickens, add a few drops of varnish to thin it out again. Clean your brush with soap and water.

TIP: Try this on jute using any color you want. It seals the jute and prevents deterioration.

 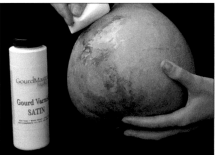 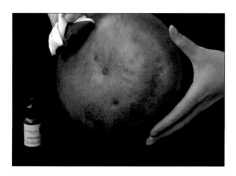

Staining a Dry, Porous Gourd

In a mixing cup with a lid, add 1 tsp. of *GourdMaster* Protective Wax and 10 drops of ink dye for a "shoe polish" like finish that is applied with a piece of felt.

Color a Dry Gourd

To successfully color a dry gourd, apply a coat of Protective Wax sparingly to seal the gourd. It will dry in minutes. Then apply inks and other coloring mediums right on the wax. This gives a true color rather than allowing the ink to soak into the gourd creating a dark surface. This is important when blending multiple ink dyes.

Protective Wax is a lightweight, high quality wax that penetrates below the surface of the gourd, sealing it and leaving a professional finish. This gourd has a protective film of wax with no color.

Ink Dye Colors

This ink is very concentrated, available in $^1/2$ fluid oz. bottles that generously color many gourds and can be mixed as desired.

The shelf life of ink dye colors is extensive.

Artprint Brown	Chestnut	Brown	Sepia	Barn Red
Cherry Red	Port Red	Pine Tree Green	Green	Olive

Violet	Mango	Orange	Yellow	Ochre	Blue	Black

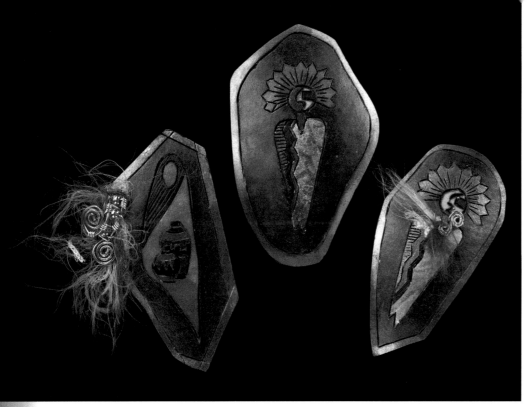

The basecoat color is Artprint Brown, finished with a mix of Red Russet Pigment Powders and Red Shimmer Glaze.

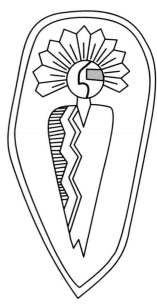

Mixing Ink Dyes

Create wonderful shimmers, metallics and translucent beauty by mixing Ink Dyes with Pigment Powders and Metallic Gel Glazes.

You'll love the elegant look of these colors.

Mixing Ink Dyes with Pigment Powders

In a jar with lid, add 10 drops of ink dye. Dip a dry brush into the pigment powder. The powder will cling to the brush. Tap powder into the ink and mix. Use a paintbrush or cosmetic sponge to apply this over your art design for a beautiful color. The powders will settle, so stir occasionally. This mix can be stored covered for weeks.

EXAMPLES:
1. Green ink dye or Pine Tree Green ink + Spring Green pigment powder
2. Crimson Red, Barn Red, Cherry Red and Port Red inks with Russet powders.
3. Chestnut ink + Bronze and Gold powders
4. ArtPrint Brown ink + Russet, Bronze, Gold, and Copper powders
5. Violet ink + Reflex Violet, Violet, and Interference Violet powders
6. Blue ink + Turquoise powder
7. Mango ink + Salmon powder
8. Yellow ink + Gold powder
9. Black ink + Carbon pigment powder
   Try mixing other combinations for more interesting colors.

Mixing Ink Dyes with Metallic Gel Glaze:

GourdMaster Metallic Gel Glaze is a creamy Gel medium with a metallic translucent glow. Mixing Gel with ink intensifies the beauty of this product and enhances the ink color beneath it.

You can also apply this mixture to a gourd by itself for a translucent finish.

This medium is very rich and concentrated so use a little at a time to minimize lines and streaks. Apply with a paintbrush or cosmetic sponge for best results. It dries very quickly.

Apply *GourdMaster* Gourd Varnish for your final finish.

PROPORTIONS:
   1 tsp. of gel glaze and 4 - 5 drops of ink
   Artprint Brown ink + Red Shimmer
Metallic Glaze or Copper Gel, Gold Gel
   Chestnut ink + Bronze Gel, Gold Gels
   Green ink + Green Shimmer Gel
   Violet ink + Amethyst Gel
   Red inks + Red Shimmer

All the ink colors mix beautifully with Shimmer White. Mix your own colors for more interesting results. Soap and water clean up while the product is wet.

Enhance this mix by adding metallic powders.

BROOCH PATTERNS
from *KK Originals Rubber Stamps*
Above #4820-G White Moon Spirit

Below #2519-G Spirit of Creativity

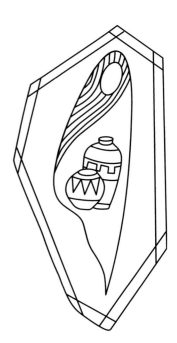

Mix wood filler with Varnish and apply with a palette knife.

Heat dry for about a minute. When the mixture turns a lighter color, it is dry.

This application is rich with color and looks just like the gourd surface.

Creating Texture

A wood filler/varnish mixture is great for adding texture to gourds, wood, clay pots, altered book art, paper, cardboard and metal.

This beautiful book cover has been textured with the wood filler/varnish mix, then colored with ink dye, pigment powders and glazes.

Wood Filler

Fill cracks and holes with wood filler as usual; air dry or use a heat tool to speed dry.

I recommend *GourdMaster* wood filler (which is not found in hardware stores). It is high quality and is designed for the arts and craft industry.

Filler from *GourdMaster* does not shrink or crack. You can sand, stain and paint over this filler for a very natural effect.

Creating Texture on a Chipboard Journal Cover

Mixing *GourdMaster* Wood Filler and *GourdMaster* Varnish together creates a very strong bond once applied to the working surface. Items that create texture include a hair comb, toothpicks, palette knife and bristles from a broom, just to name a few.

With a palette knife, scoop out 1 tbsp. of wood filler and place on a non-porous surface. Pour $1/8$ tsp. of varnish and mix. If the mix is too thin, add more filler and if too thick, add a drop more of varnish. Apply a thin layer to your surface, creating the desired texture. Let dry. Air-dry time varies.

You can speed dry with heat tool. As the filler dries, you will see the color change from Yellow to Ivory. This is now a very porous surface, so do not apply straight ink or stain. Paint this surface with the ink and varnish mix. See Staining the Raw Surface of a Gourd on page 11.

For more intense color, add 1 drop of ink at a time until you achieve the desired color. Be creative and experiment. Try sponging the ink/varnish mixture onto the surface for a different effect.

In time, wood filler may appear drier than when you first opened it. Add some varnish and it becomes creamy again. I have done this several times to the same jar and it continues to work well. After applying a base coat of color to the textured surface, all *GourdMaster* products cover this surface with a very attractive finish.

Varnish and Sand

This technique is great for landscaping, mountain ranges, pottery, desert ground, animals and so much more. You can sand off any unwanted sand after it dries.

I found the best way to do this technique is to chip carve the area just below the surface of your gourd. Fill in the recessed area with this mixture.

Varnish and Sand

Add small drops of varnish to colored play sand to create a mixture resembling grout.

Add any color ink dye to alter the sand color. This is perfect for inlaying into your gourd art.

Apply mixture with a palette knife and pack it down into the surface. A baby wipe has the perfect moisture needed to tap and pack the sand, removing some unwanted sand on the surface.

This mixture air-dries very hard in about 20 minutes or speed dry for a minute. Just varnish right over the entire gourd and sand for a final finish.

Varnish and Metallic Powders

For a beautiful metallic finish, mix $1/2$ oz. of varnish with $1/8$ tsp of metallic powder for a paint-like consistency. Add more powder for deeper color, more varnish if it is too thick.

This mixture can be stored in a covered container for weeks.

This mixture applied over a base color of ink intensifies the metallic color as it seals. You can always add a final coat of varnish when you complete your art.

Mix 1 tsp. of micro beads with 2-3 drops of varnish. This mix dries hard and strong and is perfect for filling areas for inlay and other embellishing ideas.

Place this mix in the designated area and push it to where you want it to be. The mix can be stored covered for a few weeks.

Making Your Own Templates

If desired, use template plastic and basic paper tools to create your own templates and designs.

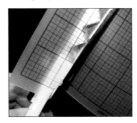

Gridded plastic template (from a quilt shop) or *GourdMaster* Designer's Template are very flexible measured grids and are perfect for creating your own rulers and templates.

Use decorative punches, small hand punches, and decorative scissors to design your own accurate, unique templates. You can easily punch right through the template plastic for perfect circles and shapes every time.

This template was made using a $1/16$" hole punch & decorative scissors. Place the template over the gourd, mark with a pencil.

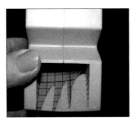
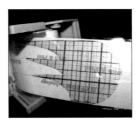
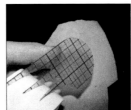
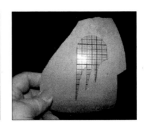

Xyron Create a Sticker machine and refill cartridges offer both repositionable and permanent stick. Using repositionable tape allows you to lift the template and change position several times. Insert it into the machine to renew the tape.

Palette Stamp and Stick Gluepad

Apply this incredible glue to a surface as the medium necessary for metal leafing, metallic powders, chalks, glitter, embossing powder and a resist. It is applied with a cosmetic sponge, a dauber, a paintbrush or with the stamp pad.

This glue glides on very easily, be sure to use just enough to cover with an even, light coat. It will be shiny at this point and it is very necessary to heat set with heat tool to activate the glue. It will change from wet and shiny to a dry sticky surface.

Apply this glue to gourds, walls for faux finishing, coated paper, and sealed porous surfaces such as wood, paper mache, glass, plastic and metal.

Tap stamp into the gluepad and stamp on the gourd. I suggest smaller stamps with less detail for successful stamping on gourds.

Always heat set this glue to activate it. Glue must become tacky so it accepts the medium you are applying.

Press leafing on the glue. Clean off excess with a sponge brush. The design stamp at left is #3927-G Alani from *KK Originals.*

Apply base color ink. dry with heat tool. Stamp in the glue pad and over the ink on the gourd. Heat set. Varnish to cancel the tack. This gives a ghost image or a very old look.

Press the stamp into the pad. Stamp on the gourd. Heat set the glue. Pour embossing powder over the glue. Heat until it embosses.

Brooch with Face

Create an original brooch from a scrap of leftover gourd. Simple add color and texture with stamps and inks.

Use *Makin's®* Air-Dry Clay and a mold from *After Midnight Art Stamps*. For a lovely effect, add pigment powders to the heat set glue. Apply multi colors if you wish and then varnish to seal your surface.

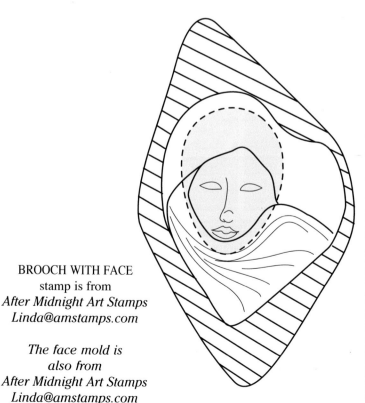

BROOCH WITH FACE
stamp is from
After Midnight Art Stamps
Linda@amstamps.com

*The face mold is
also from
After Midnight Art Stamps
Linda@amstamps.com*

Mixing White Paint with Ink Dyes

You are going to love this combination of product and you will never need to buy acrylic paint again!

Old World White Paint is an exceptional high quality paint not found in stores. It is a thicker paint and you may use a drop of extender to thin it.

About every five minutes of painting, you should rinse your brush with water and then continue painting. The reason for this is the paint tends to build up in the brush causing it to drag.

You will need a small palette or a non-porous surface for mixing. Dip your paintbrush into the White Paint and drop it on the palette.

Mix 1 drop of ink mix with the White paint to create the first monochromatic color. Add 1 drop at a time to achieve the next color.

3 drops of ink created a darker color. You will decide how dark you want the color to go. This is Cherry Red ink dye with 2 stages of color. Paint or sponge this on your surface, allow it to dry, and it usually takes about 24 hours to cure.

You do not have to wait 24 hours to continue working on your gourd but handle it gently before 24 hours to prevent scratches.

Once sealed, it will not scratch, flake or crack.

Metallic Glazes

Metallic Glazes add a beautiful metallic glow to your art.

They are translucent so if not added over a base color, they show only a hint of color. When added over a base color, the colors are more intense and a lovely complement to a similar base coat of ink.

Apply glaze to the surface with a sponge or paintbrush.

Occasionally these inks will require shaking or stirring to mix.

The applicator tip will pop off with a push and then you can insert a craft stir to stir the ink from the bottom.

Not meant to cover the entire surface as with ink dyes, metallic inks enhance the design. The opaque coverage will layer over any other color. It is easier to stain the gourd with your base color and then paint the metallic in your design.

Metallic inks clean up with water when wet and are permanent when dry.

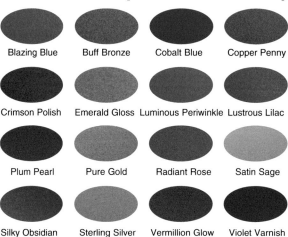

Blazing Blue   Buff Bronze   Cobalt Blue   Copper Penny

Crimson Polish   Emerald Gloss   Luminous Periwinkle   Lustrous Lilac

Plum Pearl   Pure Gold   Radiant Rose   Satin Sage

Silky Obsidian   Sterling Silver   Vermillion Glow   Violet Varnish

GourdMaster Metallic Inks

Choose from 16 Metallic Ink colors that enhance and beautify your art. These inks are completely different from the dyes so pay attention to the instructions for product use.

The ink is very thick, so apply it with a paintbrush or a cosmetic sponge.

Blue Brooch

This decorative jewelry pin shows Blazing Blue and Black permanent dye. Varnish to seal.

This lovely Native American pattern created this jewelry brooch. Embellish it with Silver wire, beads and black feathers.

Green Gourd Mask

Create this shimmering mask from a bottle gourd. Add feathers and details for an elegant look.

First layer of color is Green ink dye, over that is Green shimmer glaze.

First layer of color is Violet ink dye, over that is Amethyst shimmer glaze.

For a different color effect, try adding a few drops of ink dye into the glaze, sponge this onto the surface. Seal with varnish when you are finished.

Red Gourd Mask

Feathers enhance the texture of this mask... on the top and on the edges. Add jewels for eyes.

Use Artprint Brown as a base color for the dark areas (Brown and Red). Sponge over Red areas with Red shimmer glaze.

The light areas are White. The first coat of paint will look thin and blotchy. Air-dry for a few minutes then apply the second coat. In between, you will want to rinse your brush so the paint doesn't weigh down your brush. A third coat may be necessary and you will notice some lines as the paint dries.

Softly rub this surface with a Teflon pad to smooth and then apply your last coat. It will be smooth and very Opaque White.

Cure 24 hours for the best durable coverage, seal with varnish.

Doll with Gourd Jewelry

Sculptures of the human form have long been a favorite among artists. Create a bit of whimsy and mix in your imagination for an eclectic metallic figure that is uniquely yours.

Add texture for the hair with a blunt needle and *Makin's*® Air-Dry Clay. Color the texture with Black ink.

Rubber Stamp a sheet of *Makin's Clay* for texture on the shawl, then embellish it with *GourdMaster* metallic inks.

Cut a clay sheet in strips with scissors for the fringed skirt.

JEWELED GOURD
You may want to alter the stamp pattern slightly so it will work best on your gourd.

Geometric stamp
is from
IBrakeforStamps.com

Jeweled Gourd

Gourds are one of the oldest cultivated crops and one of Nature's greatest gifts to the artist. Often a gourd will speak to you, telling you exactly what it was born to become.

Other times you will be pleasantly surprised by the transfiguration brought about by your application of these techniques.

This is a 5" gourd. Apply tape to section on the gourd and use a macrame brass ring to trace a perfect circle around the gourd. There are several sizes of brass rings ranging from $1/2$" increments of each size.

With a pencil, trace a line around the ring. This is a guide for placing images. See pages 6 - 7 for transferring patterns.

The tape and traced ring are placement guides for aligning geometric images. Place 1 image on each of the four tape lines. This section will have 4 images evenly spaced around the gourd.

Line up the side points of the pattern to match the top point of the first set of 4 images for a total of 8 images.

 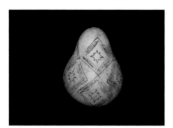  

Complete all images on gourd, adding 4 images above those done before for a total of 12 evenly spaced images.

Woodburn the images and clean the surface using Mona Lisa paint thinner. See page 7 for detailed instructions. Use an x-acto heavy-duty handle and #227 saw blade to cut along the sides of each of the four top images. See basic cutting instructions on page 5.

Remove the top of the gourd. Follow basic cleaning instructions on pages 5 -6.

Place 1 drop of ArtPrint Brown on a cotton swab. Color outside the images.

With a clean cloth, blot and smooth the color.

Heat set ink with each step of color. This prevents any ink transferring to your clothes and hands. It also sets the ink more permanently. Mango is applied to the image border.

In the smaller areas of the pattern, the microbrush is a much-needed tool. Use only a pin drop of ink and then blot on a tissue before coloring the gourd. Use a clean microbrush to remove any excess ink from this area. Wipe this brush clean with a baby wipe.

Apply Stamp and Stick from the refill bottle to the final part of the pattern. The glue is shiny when wet. You must heat set to activate the glue, which will be dull and tacky when ready.

Place Metal Leafing over the glue, smooth loose flakes with sponge brush. Save all loose flakes for the next project.

Using wire cutters, snip off the pointed tip of the tack so it is the depth of the gourd and it won't come through the other side. • Drill a hole in the center of each leafed pattern using a drill bit smaller in diameter than the tack.

Press tack into the hole. If needed, add a drop of tacky glue to the shank of tack before inserting into the hole.

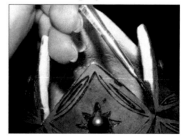

See page 13 for ink and varnish mix. Paint the varnish/Artprint Brown ink mix on the open edges to match the surface. Lightly brush over the gourd to set the ink. Wipe back and forth, removing bubbles and brush strokes, smoothing the varnish. This will dry very quickly. Apply additional coats, drying between each one.

Feather Medallion Gourd

Bold and graphic, these geometric designs make a strong,
masculine statement with traditional appeal.

Several Native American Designs embellish this large pot.

Add color with Old World White Paint and Black Ink Dye. Color the body of the gourd with Artprint Brown.

Add upholstery tacks for a nice dimension, add add jute rope handles on both sides of the gourd.

GOURD PATTERN

Turquoise Necklace

Only the highest ranking of the ancient Incas were allowed to wear the sacred stone of turquoise. Enjoy the elegant possibilities of gourd jewelry with a necklace fit for a princess.

This elegant piece has an Egyptian influence. Green inks and Green Shimmer Glaze add an antique patina.

Add copper beads and a Turquoise cabochon stone for the perfect finishing touches.

TURQUOISE NECKLACE

Triangle Necklace

Rich metallics combine in a gorgeous setting and a pendant that shimmer in any light. Dress up your day-wear or wear this stunning piece for a special evening out on the town.

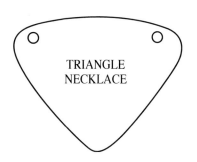

TRIANGLE NECKLACE

Eagle Necklace

Feeling self-assured today? This necklace matches your mood with bold motifs and brilliant colors.

Add a Southwest copper eagle to a recessed area on the gourd chip.

Add copper and copper wire beads to Black leather cording.

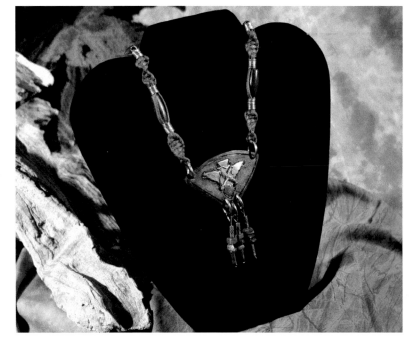

EAGLE NECKLACE

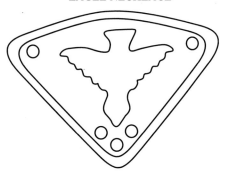

TURTLE DESIGN is from North American Indian Designs by *Dover Publications.*

TURTLE
You may want to alter the stamp pattern slightly so it will work best on your gourd.

Turtle Island Design

As a creation of nature, gourds evoke a sense of something very ancient and alive. Traditional designs magnify the feeling that this art is truly special - something to be appreciated and not to be missed.

This elegant gourd has an expression of freehand designs mixed with Native American and Turtle designs. Add rich color with Black ink and Chestnut ink.

SMALL MANDALA AND BORDER PATTERN

Trace the top half of the pattern. Rotate pattern and trace the bottom half for a complete pattern.

Mandala designs are from Mandala Designs by *Dover publications*

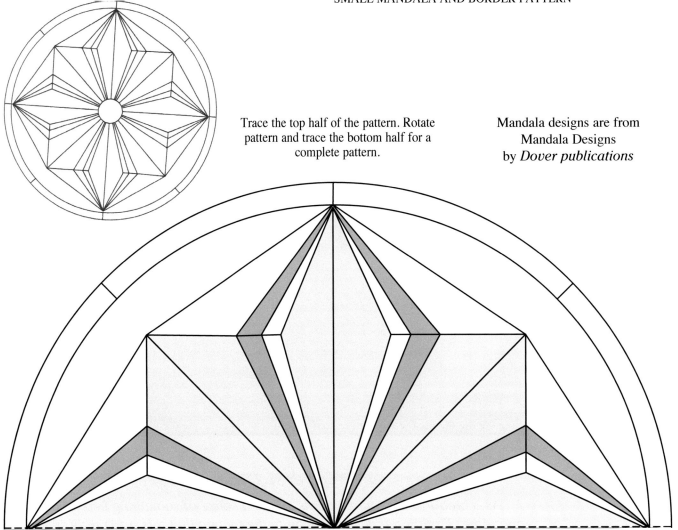

LARGE MANDALA DESIGNS are from *Dover publications*

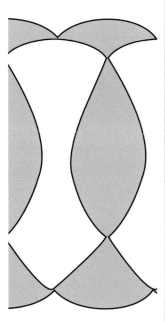

Mandala Design on Gourd

Brilliant colors in passionate tones turn a simple motif into a distinguished creation full of vibrant energy.

The Mandala design is an ancient symbol signifying unity.

First, trace the circles touching each other. Then, trace the circles centered over the originals. Recess the background of the Mandala for depth. Add color with Artprint Brown and Black inks.

Add Variegated Red Leafing for a metallic highlight. Apply Leafing with Palette Stamp and Stick Gluepad (for burnishing and rubbing).

Add texture with *Makin's®* Air-Dry Clay. Apply a border around the rim and highlight it with Metallic inks.

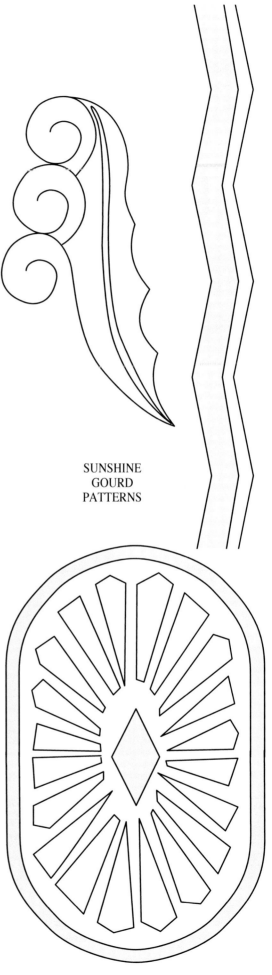

Sunshine Gourd

As the gourd changes from a natural fruit into a blissful centerpiece, it gracefully alters the life of both the artist and the viewer. Do you feel the warmth of an autumnal sun on the back of your arm?

There is something gentle in the colors and motifs presented that makes you want to reach out and touch it.

Feel the textures in the leaves, trace the flower petals. This art radiates comfort.

The small oval pattern fits in the center of the large one. Draw the large oval on your gourd first, then position the small one inside.

The missing top of this elegant gourd was perfect for adding a handle made from fibers and beads.

Add glowing color with Sepia ink and Emerald Gloss Metallic ink.

LEAF MOTIF PATTERN

Leaf stamp #25609-I is from *Magenta*

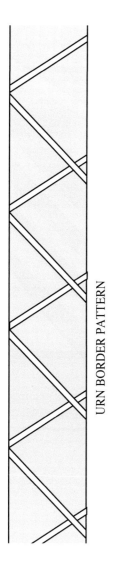

URN BORDER PATTERN

Gourd Urn

Nature crafts her pottery in an endless variety of sizes and shapes. Gourd art is all about taking something plain and making it perfect. Here, the artist has completed nature's task, transforming a simple gourd into a simply stunning vase.

Beholding this design makes one appreciate the power of combining natural materials with natural talent.

This is a true example of creativity beginning with a seed.

This beautiful design is the perfect way to show creative use of the top of a bottle gourd.

Stencil the floral design, then embellish it with metallic inks.

TRIANGLES PATTERN

TOP

Triangles Gourd

Freehand designs fill this stunning gourd with geometric patterns.

Paint the gourd with Black ink and Chestnut ink, then add Metallic accents.

TRIANGLE
DESIGN

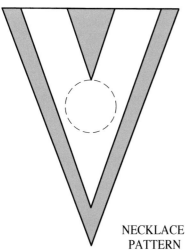

NECKLACE
PATTERN

Triangles Gourd

Swirls and symbols give motion to this delightful gourd. The seductive lines captivate one's curiosity, tempting the eye to continue its journey all around this handsome art.

Necklace

Breathtakingly bold, the wearer of this black and gold pendant is confident, strong, formidable. Wear this majestic piece when you are ready to make a statement and get noticed!

 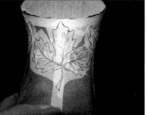 

Tape & Transfer an Image

This piece of gourd is the top cut off a large bottle gourd.

Follow Basic Taping instructions on pages 4 5. Follow Transfer Design with Masking tape. The placement of multiple leaf designs depends on the size of the gourd. The tape transfer works well because you can lift it and move it as much as you want until you are satisfied with the placement.

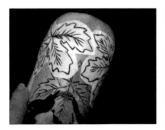  

Cutting the Gourd

Trim the excess tape so you can see how the leaves will be spaced and then wood burn all the designs and remove the tape.

Saw around the leaf designs on the upper top of gourd. This is a bit fragile because of the points and sections of leaves so I suggest using the x-acto knife with a #227 saw blade. Use the carving blade #106 to get close to the pattern.

Finish the rough edges with a sanding stick or emery board.

Coloring the Gourd

Start with 1 drop of Pine Tree Green ink dye on a cotton swab, apply ink in a circular motion on the veins of the leaf pattern.

With the same circular motion and a clean cotton swab, apply 1 drop of Artprint Brown ink dye to the area outside the Pine Tree Green and touching the Green.

On a clean cotton swab, add a drop of Mango ink. Allow it to go into the other colors. Blend all these colors together with another clean swab.

Finishing the Gourd

Heat set color for about 40 seconds.

Apply Protective wax all over the surface with a piece of felt. Wait 5-10 minutes and buff shine with a clean piece of felt.

Follow instructions to mix varnish/ink for the inside of this gourd. Once finished, add an arrangement of fall foliage to complete your gourd centerpiece.

Large Maple Leaf stamp
is from
IBrakeforStamps.com

LEAF PATTERNS

Gourd Centerpiece

Create a beautiful centerpiece for a family dinner or side table. This gourd makes a wonderful vase to hold dried florals.

This original centerpiece is the top of a bottle gourd. Only the leaves have color, and the body of the gourd is the natural color with a coat of varnish.

Fill the gourd with your choice of dried florals to complete the centerpiece.

Beaded Necklace

Heartfelt sentiments best describes this happy gourd pendant. Beaded fringe dangles complement the string for a beautiful finish.

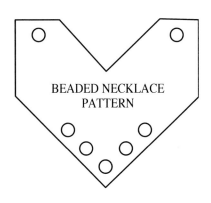

BEADED NECKLACE
PATTERN

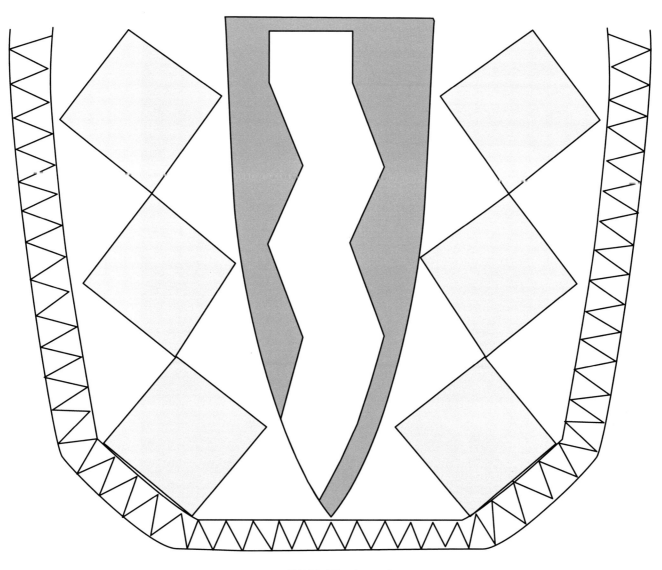

STAIR-STEP PATTERN

Stair-Step Gourd

Resplendent shimmer dazzles the eye and bewitches the senses with an opulence reminiscent of Egyptian tomb treasures. This magnificent gourd, with its irresistible texture, begs to be touched and appreciated.

Stamp diamond shapes (you can use a chunk of foam or wood as a stamp) on *Makin's* Clay. Adhere clay to the recessed area of the gourd with Tacky glue. Embellish with Metallic inks and pigment powders. See pages 14 and 17.

The zig-zag pattern on the front is worked on the original shell of the gourd. The background is recessed and painted Black.

Mother & Child Gourd

Traditional and touching, this image of Mother and Child exudes serenity.
The calm curving figures balance the strong geometric lines that complete
this composition with grace and beauty.

Create a 'V' with tape to make the area to focus the Madonna and Child.
Add Chestnut ink for the background, Black ink for the geometric freehand designs.

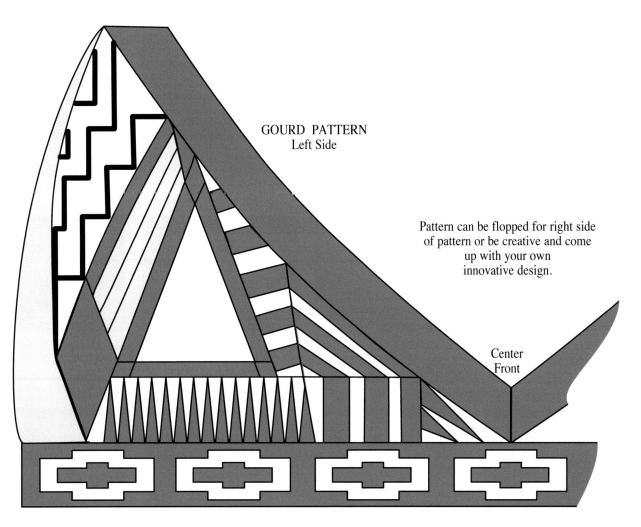

GOURD PATTERN
Left Side

Pattern can be flopped for right side
of pattern or be creative and come
up with your own
innovative design.

Center
Front

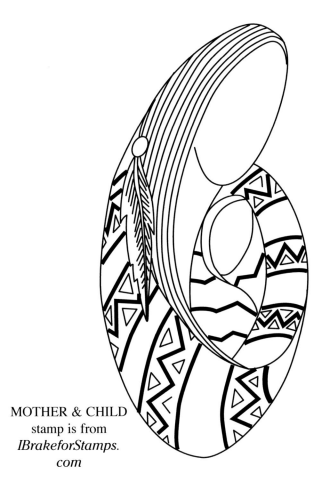

MOTHER & CHILD
stamp is from
*IBrakeforStamps.
com*

Follow Basic Taping Instructions on page 4.
Follow Basic Pattern Transfer with Masking Tape on pages 6-7. Stamp on the masking tape with Black permanent ink.
Heat set with heat tool.
Position Image on Gourd. Use macrame brass rings for tracing a perfect circle on your gourd.

Center each of the 4 designs.
Woodburn the design.
Remove the masking tape and clean the sticky residue with Mona Lisa paint thinner.
Apply Chestnut Ink all over the gourd as a stain and heat set.

Using a cotton swab and Black ink, color the first and last ring.
Apply Black ink to the pattern.
Apply Stamp and stick to the middle section of the pattern

Apply Stamp and Stick in the middle ring.
Heat set the glue until it is not shiny, 30-40 seconds.
Apply Leafing to the Stamp and Stick areas.
Remove loose leafing with a sponge brush.

Drill a very small hole with the micro drill into the center of each pattern.
Snip off the pointed tip of the tack with wire cutters so the length of the tack is equal to the thickness of the gourd. This applies only if adding the tack to an open cut gourd.
Push the tack into drilled hole in the center of each design.
Cut 9" of 16 gauge Gold wire. Create a nickel-sized coil on each end and then wrap it on the neck portion of the gourd.

Southwestern Design Gourd

Classic geometric designs are a mainstay of modern art. Express your passion in your favorite pattern. These techniques make it fun and easy.

This modern gourd is a simple project with four evenly spaced patterns.

Color the gourd with Chestnut ink and Black, then add Variegated Green Metallic Leafing.

Add an upholstery tack in the center of the pattern and on top of the gourd then coil 16 gauge brass wire around the neck.

GEOMETRIC STAMP is from *IBrakeforStamps.com*

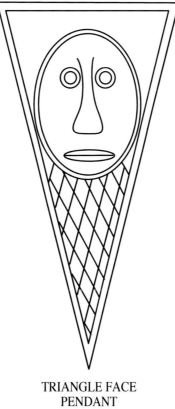

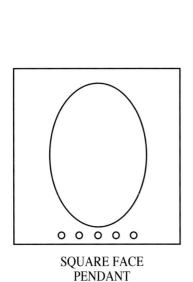

SQUARE FACE
PENDANT
PATTERN

TRIANGLE FACE
PENDANT
PATTERN

EAGLE
PENDANT
PATTERN

Triangle Face Pendants

INSTRUCTIONS:

Cut a 1" x 6" ruler from gridded template plastic.

Create checkered pattern with this ruler measuring $1/4$" increments.

Mold Black *Makin's* air-dry clay face using the *AMACO* Tribal Clay Mold. Let dry for 24 hours.

Trace face on gourd.

Woodburn this oval.

Recess this area with carving tool. See Basic Carving on pages 7-8.

Apply a few drops of Tacky Glue on the back of the dry clay face. Insert clay into recessed area on the gourd.

Seed bead border: String seed beads on a piece of 24 gauge wire cut to fit the perimeter of face.

Use a micro drill to make a few holes into the edge of the clay. Anchor the wire into the holes.

Sponge a drop of *GourdMaster* Bronze Metallic Ink to the clay face.

The gourd is colored with Chestnut ink dye and Black ink dye.

Finish with a coat of Gourd Varnish and embellish with fibers and feathers.

Gourd Pendants

Turn small pieces of gourd into exotic and exciting expressions of your imagination. Feathers, fibers, and beads maintain the natural feeling of these exquisite pieces of jewelry while the faces add expressive character.

Make the faces on these pendants with *Makin's* Air-Dry Clay and *AMACO* Tribal molds.
Add wire and beads around the faces, then embellish the pieces with feathers and fibers on the top.
TIP: The checkered pattern is drawn freehand.
The Ancient Egyptian Falcon jewelry is embellished with copper beads and feathers.

GRECIAN PATTERN

Embellish the woman and dog with metallic inks and
color the background with pigment powders.
see page 17

You may want to
alter the stamp
pattern slightly so
it will work best
on your gourd.

Grecian image is from
www.mindwareonline.com

Grecian Urn Gourd

When Michelangelo began sculpting David from a single slab of marble, he remarked that David was already present. He simply needed to chip away the marble to let him out. Much the same can be said about working with gourds. Sculpt a stunning masterpiece of your own with Maria's great techniques.

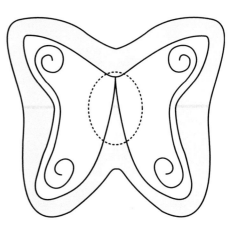

**BUTTERFLY
NECKLACE
PATTERN**

Butterfly Necklace

*Gold and turquoise delicately combine in a pendant as
beautiful an any real butterfly.*

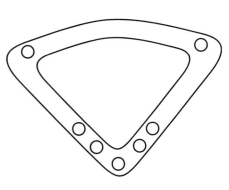

**TRIANGLE NECKLACE
PATTERN**

Triangle Pendant

*Adventurous and a little bit daring, this beaded pendant
necklace has an attitude of its own - sassy and spirited.*

Eagle Dancer Gourd

Adorn a beautiful small gourd with wire, leather lace and feathers.

Use a rubber stamp design for the Eagle Dancer, then recess the background for dimension.

Add the side pattern with a tape line, then woodburn it on both sides.

Finish the gourd with White paint and Chestnut ink dye. Add a cord into the top and embellish with fiber, wire and feathers.

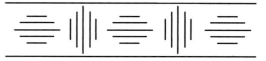

EAGLE DANCER stamp SS-80 is from *IBrakeforStamps.com*

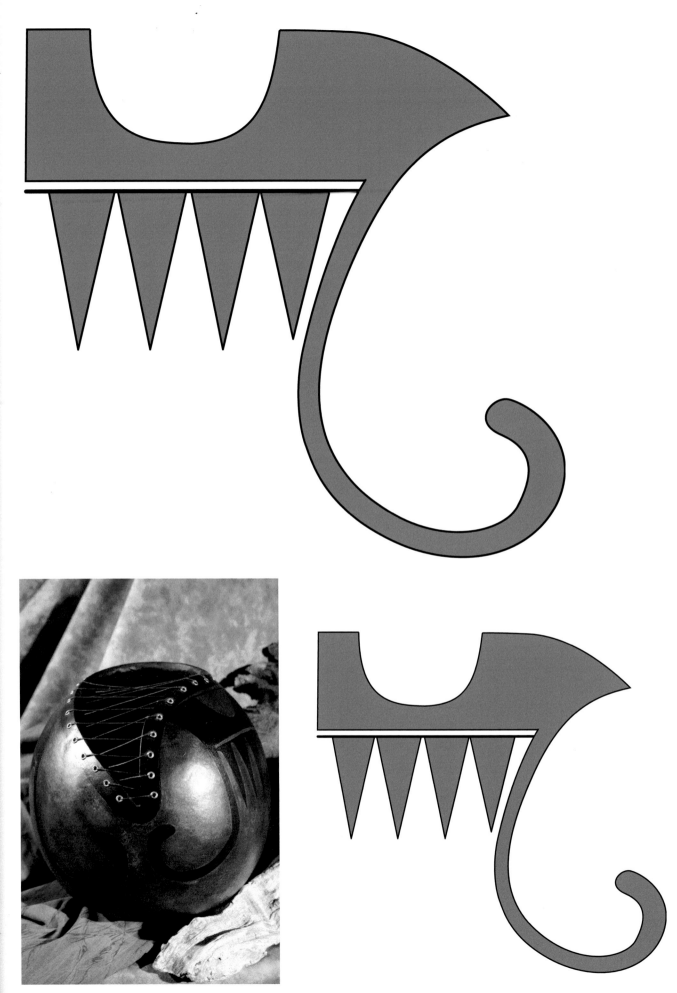

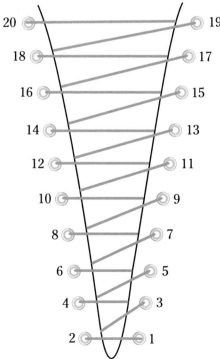

Swirl Design

Create a sense of harmony and peace in any corner of your home or place these graceful curves as the centerpiece on a table. Gorgeous gourd art enhances the beauty of any environment.

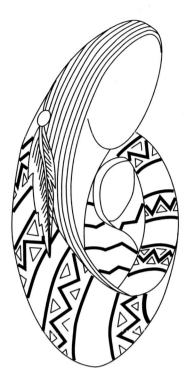

Mother & Child Pendant

Nothing gives form to the idea of perfect unconditional love like the image of a child wrapped in a close maternal embrace. Mother and Child is one of the most consistently produced themes in Western art.

The simple beauty of this pendant captivates the viewer, tenderly plucking at one's heartstrings.

MOTHER & CHILD
stamp SS-16 is from
www.ibrakeforstamps.com

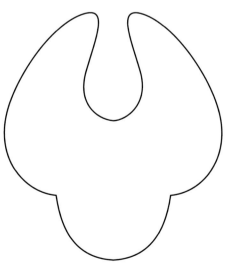

Beautiful Pendant

Appropriate for office attire and attractive as evening wear, this fabulous and feminine beaded necklace showcases an alluring gourd pendant with a beautiful stone inlay.

SCALLOPS
PENDANT PATTERN

Lacework String

'Tis a kingly gift. Vibrant hues, bold design, small nail heads, and gold threads flow together in this gourd worthy of a royal residence or palace.

Wrap Gold thread around small nails to create a fabulous and lacy design on each side of the gourd.

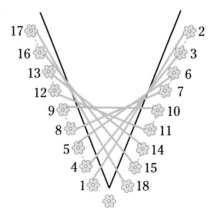

Laced Gourd

Discover the serenity of an artful experience. Softly curved strings, beads, and feathers combine with bright colors and pretty patterns in a sculpture that feels soft, warm, and soothing.

Lace wire or cord through eyelets along the edge of one side of a gourd to create a freeform pattern. Add beads to the wire or cord as you lace.

Jewelry from Scraps

Create beautiful jewelry brooches and pendants with rich colors on small pieces of gourd.

Stamp or draw design, then color and embellish the pieces as desired.

sunburst pattern on page 51
face pattern on page 40
maiden pattern on page 37